BITING THE WAX

Biting the Wax

PETER McDONALD

BLOODAXE BOOKS

Copyright © Peter McDonald 1989

ISBN: 1 85224 077 6

First published 1989 by
Bloodaxe Books Ltd,
P.O. Box 1SN,
Newcastle upon Tyne NE99 1SN.

Bloodaxe Books Ltd acknowledges
the financial assistance of Northern Arts

LEGAL NOTICE
All rights reserved. No part of this book may be reproduced, stored in a retrieval system, or transmitted in any form, or by any means, electronic, mechanical, photocopying, recording or otherwise, without the prior written permission of Bloodaxe Books Ltd.

Typesetting by Bryan Williamson, Darwen, Lancashire.

Printed in Great Britain by
Bell & Bain Limited, Glasgow, Scotland.

For Karen

Acknowledgements

Acknowledgements are due to the editors of the following publications in which some of these poems first appeared: *Gown, Honest Ulsterman, Map-Makers' Colours: New Poets of Northern Ireland* (Nu-Age Editions, Montreal, 1988), *New Chatto Poets* (Chatto, 1986), *North, Oxford Poetry, Poetry Ireland Review, Poetry with an Edge* (Bloodaxe Books, 1988), *Times Literary Supplement,* and *Verse.*

The poem 'Silent night' is based upon the true story of the imprisonment of Harold Le Druillenec, of Jersey, in Wilhelmshaven (and afterwards, Belsen) in 1944-45. His experiences were subsequently adapted into a feature programme for the BBC Home Service; the script is printed in *BBC Features*, edited by Laurence Gilliam (London, 1950).

The cover shows a detail from *A Mythological Subject* by Piero di Cosimo, reproduced by courtesy of the Trustees, the National Gallery, London.

Contents

9	The dog
10	Paprika
11	Ether
12	Short story
13	Some figures
14	Cash positive
15	Unnatural acts
19	The twilight summit
20	Count Dracula entertains (1)
21	Deception
22	A gift
23	Swimmer
25	First light
26	Pleasures of the imagination
27	Out of Ireland
28	Ideal home
29	The signal
30	The South
31	Killers
32	Christmas
33	In the hall of mirrors
34	Silent night
39	Fire
40	Grace before meat
41	Consequences
42	A Short History of the World
43	Survivors
44	Prospectus
46	China
47	A volume of memoirs is forthcoming
48	Mahogany
49	Still life
50	A prism
51	Tercets
52	The deaf wars
53	Totalled
54	Count Dracula entertains (2)
55	The third day
56	The green, grassy slopes of the Boyne
58	Sunday in Great Tew

The dog

The dog lay there with one leg missing,
dead apparently, right in front of the door
all morning. We came out to move it,
but a crowd from somewhere catcalled and hissed,
then a stone or two clattered past us, hit
the window, took a chunk out of the wall.
We retreated, and the dog still lay there.
Silence from outside echoed in the hall.

That night, it was dogs barking everywhere,
glass crunching on the road. The TV
spat and flickered for an hour or more
until the pictures stopped, as suddenly
as the lights blacked out and the phone died.
Inside, we fumbled out matches and candles
and just made out the windows shaking, handles
tried on the strong doors. Then voices outside.

The restless natives wouldn't show their faces
until the very last, so it was said.
The only time they'll look you in the eye –
patterns of plaster on the sheepskin rug –
it's then you'll know that you're as good as dead.
Still carpeted, the flat had felt like a safe place
most days, although at night the noises started
and the locks got stronger. Now there was the dog.

At last, peace: dawn and a spreading silence,
fires burning out, maybe a car passing
and little else to be heard. By midday
one of us had ventured out, was standing
on the littered path, swiping the flies away.
The dog was there still, and the smell of the dog.
He called back, *An accident*. In the distance
a helicopter with one blade missing.

Paprika

Behind them, the radio surges
its way into the conversation.
Early evening, and the noise of Europe
is Babel's atmospherics,

the sound of dust and headaches.
Rising in the half-dark
they close a window, make coffee,
try to hold down the signal...

Florence this summer. And next
year somewhere new – down
the Rhine, Hungary maybe,
or that tour of Yugoslavia.

The birds are deafening, the radio
white noise by now, and even
the coffee is burning their tongues.
Something terrible is going to happen.

Ether

Those lovers in the attic
who scratch and cry their way
out of each other's lives
gradually the night through
until, at dawn, they sleep,
are becoming the soundtrack
for the worst of our bad dreams,
our separate B-movies
where the lumbering, hurt monsters
turn out to be ourselves.

I look inside your lovers' heads
to where you lie naked,
frozen blue on the soil,
and lurch away in terror
through mist and huge trees,
still hearing the first of your cries,
your moans, and gasps, and silences.
A brute, my hands fumble
from trunk to trunk, as if
the damp wood kept you there.

Kneeling at a rain pool
and about to catch the water,
I can tap your snow-dream
through fathoms of ether;
silence, but for the crack
and groan of ice
further and further north;
some creature's wounded howl
for a face that shatters
at the drop of one hand.

Short story

At last there was time to dream again,
or it seemed that way at least.
The sunset had changed only slightly
since yesterday, but it had changed.

The photograph he tried for became
a letter, and the letter became ash
in his own hearth before long,
even before the sun had set.

There was always something else to be caught,
or there would be soon, with luck.
His fire burned like the sun in Florida

where, slightly drunk by now, the last
astronaut alive was still wondering
how to make his way back to the moon.

Some figures

The clouds were following one another south
and we were following the clouds, as if
that were the reasonable thing to do,
slowly for days, then slowly for a month,
feeling the ice begin to lace our breath
like men who had already come to grief
and were buried now in air and sea-snow.

But pressing on required no special skill;
the nights were full of drink, the days morose
and broody, staring down to a thick sea,
awaiting the day of arbitrary landfall,
then wading ashore in ones and twos, until
we stood, wrapped up like spacemen, close
together, in ourselves a single colony.

I think perhaps we wanted to begin again,
to have another try at that new start,
but the ice and sleet, as we huddled there together,
were making for cohesion, and the pain
involved in staying close seemed less in vain
than that of separation, being torn apart
to strike out freely, far from one another.

And so we stayed, and froze into our places
as snow-sculptures, first with faces half-defined,
then bolder, heavier forms with curious features,
and finally as abstract things, where traces
of figure or line are conjectural, and surfaces
are white and changing, leaving nothing behind
to hold us all accountable as living creatures.

Cash positive

Two telephones all morning giving each other hell
in the highest office between here and God,
a desk polished black so you can see your face
and a silent screen that flashes messages

across cities, oceans and thousands of miles;
a printer beside it zipping away, murmuring
at intervals all day in different inks;
nobody says much except to the telephones.

I'd start by talking about securities,
though nobody is ever safe, and things
get sticky, dangerous – you might even
pick up something nasty from the keyboard

or the one love of your life, just think of that.
And what reply *is* there anyway
to the fax's cruel jibing, its clever *This
is the promised land calling, the poor boy on the line*?

Unnatural acts

1. *Still*

Clutching his sides at the very mention of the name,
he looks, caught there, as though he might be
preparing either to laugh or to cry his heart out.

Around him most of the others are stony faced,
fixing their gazes on a point some seven feet
from the floor on the one wall that isn't there.

Only the dark-haired girl is beginning to respond,
raising spread palms, opening her eyes wide
and training them just clear of his left shoulder.

Although there's no sign as yet of the unexpected guest
inside the frame, he'll still be around somewhere,
keeping close to the wall, probably, just about here.

2. *Wrong*

Even if she had asked him, the blue girl, what
she might say or do just at that moment
or how she could ever ask the right way of things,
even if the music had stopped, or at least
had become softer, then there might have been a chance;
as it was, the spotlights flashed over her cheeks,
over her shoulders and back, the blue of her hair,
the music dropped down on top of her like lead
and down from the ceiling a thousand lethal
bubbles came floating, then confetti and streamers
came down and burned her, everything, even
the lights and the cold were pointing to the same
conclusion, and then of course her colours changed;
even the doorman was seen to wipe a tear
away with the finger of one white glove,
as if, with that gesture, he too might bring the house down.

3. Galatea

Each night when they bring her face to face
with her torturers, when she
and the branding iron come cheek to cheek,
he's in his box, watching from behind a curtain,
and before retrieving his coat and top hat
from the headless lackey, will have closed
his eyes just as she and the hot iron
kiss, opening them in time for her screams
and the rest of the action, live on stage.

Is he quite sure she felt no pain?
Alone at night in his private chamber
of horrors, locked in with her waxwork double,
he gives his doctor's hands
the run of her body, smoothing out
blemishes and talking as a lover might do,
allowing himself one classical allusion
as he starts to unbutton Galatea's dress,
biting the wax, abject, *surréaliste*.

4. *Dead*

We spent that morning talking to the dead men.
After the first drink and before the last
it came to me that maybe they were telling
less than the whole truth. There was, for instance,
the question of how she'd managed to escape,
or just how much she'd tell, given the chance,
and, given the choice, which of us would be trusted?

The room had one big window, wall to wall;
we might have been swimming right into the clouds,
high as so many kites. I pressed the matter,
asking this one and that for a straight version:
at best, all I got was a sorry grin
and a nod or a wink through an empty bottle,
but I was pushing on to the bottom of this.

One of them hit a button on the video
for no apparent reason; the screen was white
with glancing sun, we paid it no attention,
and I was on the point of another question
when the whole room started to fill with murmurs
of recognition, for there she was, with two
of our very best performers, giving her all.

Out of a hundred things there to admire,
what took my fancy was the red of her nails
pressing his white skin, and that look of terror
in all their eyes at once. Coming to later,
baking in light under the big window,
I lifted the receiver and made arrangements.
They were right, the dead men. That girl would go far.

The twilight summit

Imagine the scene:
it's one of those places in Donegal
where the Volvos never bother to stop,
and this pub's more of a dance-hall
that's empty, near enough, all afternoon;
a cave for drinking in,
a cave of making and dreaming,
more real than O'Hagan's paper-shop
or the road from here to Bundoran.

A pair of hardened *raconteurs*
are busy finding the words
to measure the distance between them:
each leans and leers towards
a bar where the different ambers
of two pints dwindle, beside them
each a glowing talisman
of Bush or Jameson's,
where nation speaks unto nation.

By now, those hoarse, raised voices
are echoing so much
around this blacked-out dance-floor
that neither of them really hears
what it is the other's saying.
There's one last lunge and clutch
at a glass, and here comes more,
though nobody knows who's paying.
Good man yourself, then. Cheers!

Count Dracula entertains (1)

Unfortunately, it was never simple,
though for years now you've been dreaming
of wonderful solutions. Did I scare you?
I have this habit of coming through
just at the wrong time, like other things,
hunger, love, sleep for example.

Forgive the accent: you will understand
what it's like to be a foreigner abroad
or, for that matter, an alien at home,
where you curse it all, to the last bomb
waiting its moment on some empty road
that stretches out into the back of beyond

– which is my country too, of course,
completely surrounded by one blank sea
we call oblivion, despair.
Maybe one day you could spend some time there:
it's just the place to write your poetry,
to go to the bad, and then to worse.

Our comforts, I'm afraid, will be few
and simple, but you'll still have your visions
– a tree of light, then nothing but light –
and I'll still have my victims every night,
for ours would be the finest of collusions:
the best dreams are of dreams coming true.

Deception

The narrow channel they call Neptune's Bellows
leads into Whaler's Bay, a lava beach
where tin cans from the fifties and big bones
are leftovers with few now to disturb them
along the dull fringes of Deception Island.
Mostly the penguins come and go, often
a conclave of fur seals makes an appearance,
and sometimes you can pick out human figures
among the oil tanks and dead furnaces,
like wanderers with nowhere left to go
who wind up here, the last place on God's earth.
They'll be scientists, perhaps, or crazy tourists
on a trip from Cape Horn to the South Shetlands,
viewing the litter and the whaling relics
in summer weather. They leave their marks, too:
soft drink and vodka bottles, petrol cans,
or bold graffiti written out in Spanish,
signatures scattered among the other last things
where a rock by the sea reads *Death to Pinochet.*

A gift

The maker of necklaces turns his back
on the latest customer. Before
you go, take this: silver and black,
a string of glass from London,
hand-worked silver, pebbles black to the core.

In the car doing ninety,
England is peaceful, the past
no more than a minute's sky,
neutral, nothing to do with us.
We stop to the smell of petrol
and hot rubber, home at last.

With my one hand holding a glass,
the other ponders the intricate
weight of your necklace.
For a moment, I hesitate
before I speak, at one almost
with the heat of four black tyres,
the sky, the smell of petrol,

with the customer, and the maker of necklaces.

Swimmer

Stung, twisting in
and out of himself, he
gapes into the current,

swallowing its weight
to drag himself down
into a dark continent,

an unmapped green
tortured with voices,
opening up, closing

over him. He can hear
his own voice bubble:
everything is possible

and probable;
for the dreamer, there are
no secrets, no illusions,

no laws. His fish-
eye could let her swim
back into the world

holding the tiny
pebbles of Valium
safe in her palm.

The writing on her letters
runs, a hard smear
over the roof of light

that splinters as
he dives upwards,
gasping in the air

of the place where she waits
for a stranger
to come from the water

into the summer heat
and a dull
mirage-shimmer

over the riverbank.
He climbs to a place
where everything is possible

as the sky levels
its long blue spaces
into a dream of water.

First light
(Euripides, *Phaethon*)

Already, on the hills,
men are at work, tending
animals and whistling softly
to themselves. In a field
nearby, two horses
crop the grass lazily.

Elsewhere, coming out
of hiding, the professional
hunters have won again.
They rest in a clearing
and light cigarettes
as blood steams in the sun –

a neutral light
and silence that could yet
fill with music;
the alien sweetness
of nightingales (there has
been talk of violence,

madness); or the swan's
last aria coming through
from springs high up
where fresh water
will break from rock
when the death-song is over.

About a mile off coast
a single yacht is leaning
into the spray.
Its sails fill
with the whole weight of morning
as it turns away.

Out of Ireland

Just how far do you have to go
before you get to the world's edge?
Today, a hard sun lights the snow
for miles, and deep inside his cage

your tame canary sings and dances,
ignoring winter. He has a voice
and uses it, taking no chances.
He entertains, as though he had a choice.

This summer you'll be sailing west,
whether the sea is calm or angry,
until you drop. Your bird knows the rest,
he knows he'll die hungry.

Pleasures of the imagination

Again I'm caught staring
at the sky, in particular
those blue-black clouds
that shadow the sun. I remember
I was meant for a painter
and see in a puddle
cause for reflection.

I've packed my bags again
for cloud-cuckoo land;
you might see me there,
mouth agape, as I recline
on beds of asphodel,
finally reaping the benefits
of a classical education.

But there are other approaches;
the celebrated Donal O'Sheugh
owes his allegiance
to a different culture.
He has carpeted his apartment
in the heart of New Jersey
with the best Irish turf

(perhaps, all the time,
he was speaking in parables).
Not that it matters –
I think I could stay here
amazed by this September
sun-shower, quite silent,
until his cows come home.

Meanwhile, on a deserted
film-set, the handsome
Count Dracula has heard tell
that he is a metaphor now,
and is unhappy.
He aspires to symbolism
and perhaps, one day, to nothing at all.

Ideal home

As soon as you open the front door
on to a deep-pile hall carpet
and harvest-gold walls,
you begin the new life.
In the lounge, you sit
smoking, as your wife
fixes some drinks, maybe cocktails.
Already you're asking for more.

It's been like this from the start;
a kitchen that almost runs itself,
the TV, the sleeping video.
In case of emergencies
the basement has enough
food for twenty days,
a purring clock-radio
and an ash-tray the shape of a heart.

The signal

It seemed too long to wait, and the queue, a dozen deep,
barely moved in half an hour, so he took his hat and left,
went to open the glass door to the traffic and the people
in their winter coats and beards, when the man behind him laughed

and he looked and there behind him was another beard and coat
and another and another, and the heavy glass sighed shut,
for the people would not look, and he knew that he'd been caught
when the men came into focus with their faces grey like slate.

But the queue itself was silent, and he wondered whether now
it was time for him to speak, to ring a bell or cry for help,
but he kept his mouth shut all the same, because he knew
that the orders and sub-clauses in his case gave no hope.

No hope for him of moving any further now than back
to the queue of coats and beards, this time to the very end,
and his own face was like slate, and the slate about to break,
and the pieces when they broke would fall away and not be found.

So he stood his ground like Simeon, his beard began to grow
as the rain blattered and blurred the glass world of the door
where no one spoke or moved, and the light stopped coming through
when his silence rose in silence, broke in darkness like a flare.

The South
(for Campbell Gemmell)

The story may not be true, of course: that pair
who'd lived too close to an airbase, or seen one
too many documentaries where bombs
exploded a mile over the dome of St Paul's;
panicked, they hauled an atlas from the shelf
and searched out data on prevailing winds,
on rainfall, tides, and all the likely targets.
They came up with a location far to the south
as the safest place in either hemisphere,
sold up and moved there, having chosen then
(a year before that episode was played)
the Falkland Islands in the South Atlantic.

Each time you hear that easy parable
it changes, gains or loses from the teller,
his sense of detail, or her sense of timing
(a lot, of course, depends upon the punchline).
The best response to a story is to cap it
with a better of your own; let's say the year
you found yourself on ice, much further south,
in the shifting deserts of Antarctica;
the Chilean aeroplane refuses to land,
so here you stay, stuck at a weather station,
listening for the news from the Malvinas,
a thousand miles from here to anywhere.

Killers

You could think of them as hunters,
achieved, professional,
ready for anything.
Their minds are on the job in hand
and their hands are steady.
They've gone by now, most likely,

but in the country, one by one,
the birds are falling
out of the trees, into
another shade of green;
just sparrows, thrushes,
nothing exceptional,

at least nothing you'd notice
in this weather, walking
the wet road home
at closing time, until
there are hands on your arm,
light as feathers.

Christmas

The spaceship drifting up
from the ground to the second floor
of the Belfast Co-op
to ferry me and a dozen others

into the presence, slides home
and unloads me, while
my tight frown fixes
each request exactly

for him to hear and remember.
He takes me on his knee
and offers, to go on with,
a yellow plastic steamship.

Later it occurs to me
that somehow he is able
to appear in more
than one place at a time,

for he suffers the little children
in five or six stores daily.
But in mysteries like this
everything is possible:

him riding in the air
through a night speckled
with snow-fluff, or Michelin
spacemen in orbit,

their cracked despatches
indecipherable; even the child
my mother never had, waking
early on Christmas morning,

who finds his presents waiting
at the foot of the bed
exactly as he dreamt them,
and begins to smile.

In the hall of mirrors

To think that it should come to this,
seeing my own eyes look me in the face
where the bigger I get the smaller I become,
vice versa, in a flash. Nobody said
anything about this, or what it's worth
to you, or me, or anyone.
And how many mirrors would they need,
how few could they get away with?

The strip-lights flicker up like nerves
on all the miles of motorway
through the skulls of these giants and dwarfs,
assorted spooks and goons; but why
should my feet be rhyming with my head
on glass, like razor-blades with spoons?

Silent night
(St Aubin's Bay, Jersey, 1946)

It's summer now, or nearly. Out at the back door, my sister
shows the children how to feed the birds, scattering pieces
of crust into the garden: some sparrows, a couple of starlings
come down and squabble, fly off at the children's applause.
In the bathroom, I'm weighing myself – another stone – smiling,
hearing my name called, catching the smells from the kitchen.

Those weeks when they came to take my story for the wireless
I had to be coaxed at first; they seemed to be after
more than names, or names and facts; they wanted to know
how it felt then, and sounded, what it tasted and smelt like,
though really it was like nothing, nothing before or since,
which I told them, and they understood, they said. But even so.

But even so, as they added, there was a story to be told,
and I was the man to tell it. First, there were questions
and answers, *What did you see then? And what were you thinking?*
But after a while, the story would come out of its own accord
and there were the details they wanted, the smells and the sounds,
memories that had never made sense, for once locking into each other.

The first place they took you. At Wilhelmshaven that winter,
when every afternoon repeated the frost of that morning
and at night there was only hail to cut into the tracks
of their lights, they bundled me with a couple of dozen
newcomers into one of the big huts, my feet touching
the ground for the first time since the court-martial in Jersey.

How many in this hut? There were nearly a thousand,
crammed three to a bed, head to toe in the bunks and making
barely a sound. Near enough a thousand men. Packed
that tightly, you soon learn to sleep without moving,
and you learn not to speak, you learn to lie still and say nothing
when there are guards on hand to force up the value of silence.

It was part of Neue Gamme, and I'd been brought over
from France with the others – Jean De Frotté, Bernard
Depuy, just to give two names as examples: the first one
tall, wispy-haired and delicate, the son of a Marquis,
then Bernard with his square head screwed down on to his shoulders,
though they have their own stories, parts of mine and still different.

We had three things to talk about: food, sleep and work,
but no real need to think, for they were all taken care of,
especially the last. Once a day, there was thin turnip soup
and a crust of bread, a few hours of motionless sleep,
then the hard tramp through frost out to the Kriegsmarine
Arsenal, a day's work hearing the punch and clang of the riveters,

avoiding the welders' blue clouds of sparks; sweat and iron;
then our convicts' shuffle back to the camp in the dark,
their searchlights tailing us and filling in the distance
back to the gates, our hut with its three hundred bunks.
I mentioned guards: there were guards of course, but worse
were the Chiefs, one to each hut. Ours was called Omar.

You might ask me to describe, explain him, but I can do neither,
I can tell you his build, his features, even mimic his voice,
but that would add up to nothing, or nothing more really
than just a man in a story, maybe a bit of a monster,
a dead man anyhow. Yes, by now he'll be safely dead.
It might be easier, really, for you yourself to explain him.

Omar, it turns out, had once, like most of the others,
been a prisoner himself, a young man when they caught him
in 1933, some kind of radical journalist.
He'd been through worse than this in his time, worse beatings,
work, cold and the rest, and he was in for a lifetime.
Drop by drop, I suppose, the fight just bled out of him.

So by the time the camps were getting busy they made him an offer,
to serve his time as an *Alteste* in places like Neue Gamme
with at least enough freedom there to do as he pleased
and get on with the job. Yes, the words apply, brutal, sadistic,
just like the others, inhuman. And yes, there are stories.
I try to remember my friend Bernard's straight talking,

'There's no point in judging a place like this by the standards
of what we've all left behind: it has a code of its own,
a lunatic code, I know, but you just have to learn it.
Lie still and say nothing.' So what is there for me to say now
about Omar? Just the truth, just what I remember?
But I couldn't call it the truth then, and now that I tell you

the stories, does that make them all true? does it make them
happen, happen properly for the first time? It's harder,
watching the sea relax under the first mild summer evening
and waiting for dinner, too, harder to force those things
to happen again, and here, than just to keep silent. And lie?
Here by the bay, there's really no such thing as silence,

what with the waves breaking all night, and the seabirds
carrying on as usual each day. On the wireless, they tell me,
you can do wonders, but the one thing you can't get away with
is silence, the fretful noise of empty spaces, the worrying
gaps bare of music or talk, with just the sound of the atmosphere
coming into your very own room. I can give you two stories

concerning Omar, though whether or not they go well together
I myself couldn't say. The first happened only a few weeks
after we arrived at the camp: an Alsatian boy of sixteen
had been caught making off with some scraps of food from the plates
of patients in the infirmary (though that was hardly a hospital
as you'd understand the word – a dirty, crowded tin hut).

He came up before Omar, of course, who glared and let his face buckle
in on itself with disgust, then brought out the worst of his voices,
the fabulously wicked giant, to himself above all.
'You, boy,' he thundered down, 'you have committed
the one unforgivable crime; you have gone out and stolen
not only from your comrades, but from your sick comrades.

I'll tell you exactly how you can expect to be punished:
you're going to be made to learn the real meaning of hunger,
but you'll dread the food in your mouth; and when you leave us
you'll be raving mad, boy, gibbering away somewhere to die.'
He was perfect. Large as life and more monstrous than any
caricature. We kept quiet; the boy cringed, was carried away.

The usual stamping, shouting and beating. Then the wet blankets
to sleep in as well, for nights on end. They starved him,
then force-fed him salted food, served up on a scalding
hot spoon, day after day, all the while refusing him water.
By the time they finally lost interest, he looked like a skeleton;
unable to eat for the burns on his mouth, his scarred lips and tongue,

he would scream at the sight of a spoon. He died soon, of course,
raving mad, as Omar had promised. Now I can barely imagine
such things happening at all, but they did, and do still
in theory, in places far removed from this island,
the standard horrors, common knowledge now more than ever,
more than just hearsay these days: newsreels, words on the air.

And then of course there's the second *vignette*: the very same Omar
– who was, needless to say, cultured, had once been a classical
musician, to add to his attributes, always a lover of Mozart –
in the Christmas of '44, Omar's treat for the prisoners.
Imagine one of the huts that's been specially cleared for the purpose,
with benches there now and a stage, the audience all silent

(though you'd hardly mistake that silence for hushed expectation,
it being clearly enough the schooled silence of fear)
and then you make out a Christmas tree just to the right of the stage,
a piano likewise, the feeling of something about to begin.
Then suddenly Omar and the six other *Altesten*
troop on like schoolboys, heavy, bloated, all with straight faces.

For this is the carol service, and these fat men are the carollers.
Listen and you'll pick up easily Omar's gentle booming
among all the voices here. In fact I myself was arrested
for 'communal listening'; the whole thing happens again for the
    wireless,
but no actor alive could reproduce the sound of this memory,
that music in the hungry air, *Stille nacht, Heilige nacht*.

On clear evenings, I watch those rocks on the near side of the bay,
a circle of broken teeth, finally blotted out by the tide.
I listen to seabirds roosting for miles along the whole coastline,
and then there's just the sea noise and the evening programmes
with the bad and the good news, the music of Victor Sylvester,
the Epilogue, the King, the whisper and fizz of the atmosphere.

Some nights I almost see the dead and the living stand in a circle,
naked but for their memories, and in full view of each other,
immobile as those rocks crumbling gradually into the bay,
as though they were trying to speak, or cry, or scream in the silence,
to hear each other and understand; but the dead weight of stone
holds us all down, makes us stand still and say nothing.

But not when they call me to dinner, and I laugh with the children
over this or that story, though sometimes I'll catch myself thinking,
not of the past exactly, but more of that programme,
my voice and the voices of actors, and somewhere among them
Jean and Bernard alive; Omar's Christmas carol; the last
winter of a bad war; a boy with a horror of spoons.

Fire

Sometimes, Le Druillenec, I try to imagine you
waiting for the man from the BBC,
wearing a grey suit, a fresh shirt, the blue
tie that was a Christmas present. There will be
seagulls overhead, and on the radio
a band playing wartime favourites; the glass
in your hand will go warm, your smile will show
him nothing but welcome, leaving him to guess
at silenced depths of memory or sorrow.

Reading the words he helped put into your mouth,
I try to make out gaps in the conversation
between you, those few weeks when he came south
to Jersey to test his own imagination
against the unimaginable: bare, lethal names,
Neue Gamme, Belsen, shunted into history
or pitched into the atmosphere. Nobody blames
you for your reticence, able now to see
how your shy smile is both generous and sane.

In Ireland late this summer, I climbed high
enough up Slieve Donard to see out
along the coast for miles; a neutral sky
had nothing down there to be concerned about
as I sat in the sun above it all,
cupping the brittle water in my hands.
Light touched the mountainside with fire, and tall
cloud-shadows shifted quietly; a dry stone wall
settled in on itself and the feel of high ground.

Harold Le Druillenec, whether you're living or dead,
I want you to come with me. When the sun turns
a corner of the mountain, and touches my head,
say nothing about that French boy with the burns
on his lips and tongue. Tell me instead
how this silence can be spoken; help me understand
the intricate geography of all islands,
the tricks of distance; stand close, help me find
out once and for all the lie of the land.

Grace before meat

A spoon palms, cups her face,
her whole body
displaced on the surfaces
of cutlery. The table
is a written page

where now the knives
might be glancing back at me,
seeming to smile
in the light that carves its way
from edge to clean edge.

Consequences

I must be about fourteen or fifteen,
for I seem to be walking through wet
sunlit streets with Andy and Stephen,
and trying to look older than I am,
say seventeen or eighteen, with luck.

Music is pulsing out like morse
to Ann Street and the world
as we flaunt its loud new colours
where later, relishing the danger,
the three of us might share a can of lager.

*

Years ago, in the redbrick school
at Gilnahirk, that spring day
when the master, Mr Peterson,
finally gave Tom Boyd the strap,
the strongest of us winced to see

his hands close on their weals
as he learned his lesson, gradually.
There was something resembling sympathy
in our faces then, but not for long.
Tom Boyd was fat. We hated him.

*

Another one of those long parties
I couldn't get out of. My glass
needs a refill; Dr Stephens
and Mrs Andrewes are addressing themselves
to the question of public sponsorship

for the opera; I must be talking
to a girl who looks nineteen or twenty
about her painting, *The Toy Shop*,
when suddenly our shy host, Mr Morse,
is asking will I step outside one moment.

A Short History of the World
(for John Hughes)

It begins with another *non sequitur*,
a man and a woman talking,
getting nowhere fast. They're sure
of one thing only, that they're walking,
however slowly, right out of the picture,
just that one thing.
It follows, by and large, from there,
until the man in the hat walks in,
saying he's just come back from the interior.

The rest is history again, in fact
his starring role of 1948
in MGM's *Short History of the World*
(a flop), another film or two, then back
to the first obscurity. Tonight's late
movie shows him at his best though,
out in the cold and on the run,
cornered apparently in a blind alley
and trying to strike dud matches in the rain.

Survivors

Next morning, we slip back out
to the garden to gather up.
Sluggish ghosts of cigarettes
are still losing their grip
on the rooms they used, where now
like inoffensive flags,
failures, thin curtains flap.

We've cleared inside, somehow,
hangovers notwithstanding,
seen the glasses gathered in
and swept disaster-zones
where they tried out their crash-landings,
we've corralled the dead and dying
bottles, and poured away the dregs.

Lastly, the garden here:
damp grass and tramped-in fags,
half-empty beer cans, top-
heavy trees, the sun going in.
Ten minutes more of ending
it all, and the last one standing's
a pushover, a spilt glassful of rain.

Prospectus

In front of me, like stones, the consequences
stretch to where my eyes stretch, and further,
clear suddenly and suddenly gone again,
with words there I can almost decipher:
they could be distances, or maybe names
found and lost, chances and second chances.

I have brought her back into an old house
where a wall leans slightly, and the roof carries
its weight of clouds under a north sky.
I spell her name in ivy and dark berries
over the lintel, asking her to stay
as evening lifts towards us from the grass.

On the mantelpiece, all the sepia dead
are drifting from their frames out into shadows –
straight Victorian faces, an army of children,
strong, awkward farming men and tired widows
with nothing left to say, who seem to file
together into the strict dark of their God.

When I turn my back on them and light the stove
her face starts to come clear again, repeats
its pagan message, *love me.* Just yesterday
we drove the coast road to a rainy beach,
and beyond the plastered windscreen was the sea,
taciturn, blunt, and grudging every wave.

As the sun dropped over that hard coast
we drove inland, me naming every town
for her, re-telling all my father's stories
and maybe inventing a couple of my own
full of his characters and stage-properties,
his comic country with a roguish cast,

and found myself half-trusting what I told her,
the words as clear as lamps, marking the road home.
But we know that we can visit here just once,
and that making love tonight is where we start from,
implying distances, a string of plunged stones,
graves and miles, one day following another.

China

Just as he'd told them every Christmas,
her father would be dead within the year.
She would marry again within another
and move to a different neck of the woods.
The brother and his wife would have their second daughter.

Distances grew vaster every year:
his death had brought the father no closer,
and her brother came no nearer a son,
so at last the name, too, would go.
Now there was no more really to be done

than to meet up each year at Christmas,
or maybe just every other Christmas,
when they would talk, and she might mention
something of what it was she was after
when the job let her get away,

and even, if the words didn't fail her,
how she had gone the length of China
and walked on the wall
fully a mile
quite recently, just the summer before last.

A volume of memoirs is forthcoming

And now they tell me that the old girl's dying,
stuck on the West coast with that bad third son
who's helping her rewrite the will again;
apparently she's hired some young gun
to ghost the memoirs she's been threatening
for longer now than even I remember.
At nights she sits up with a tape-recorder
and spits out memories like bitter seeds,
pointing the finger, naming all the names,
telling it like it is, or was, or needs
to be in the long run. Each sick morning
when she's back on her deathbed, and the beads
are clicking away in the bedroom, he sits down
and listens through the night's fresh revelations;
then it's back to tapping words across a screen,
watching the evidence accumulate
in hard green letters, irrefutable.

It can't be long now till the thing's in print,
and I'll be combing the index for my name,
morose and sullen, tight-lipped, miserable,
watching as she helps me to the blame
for everything, for almost everything.
Sometimes I'll wake, much as I do these nights,
and catch in the dark above me a quick glint
from her one green eye, and maybe hear her sing
snatches of ballads that I'd never learn
at her knee, or at the hearthstone; then I'll turn
my face to the wall and shout her ghost down:
already, you see, I've got her in my sights;
I have the material ready now and waiting,
and I start writing tomorrow at dawn.

Mahogany

They drink cold wines by the side of a river
as respite from their table talk, while under
planted trees the quiet flunkeys gather
comparing notes, half-trusting one another.
It is nearly safe for us to leave them there.

They rise refreshed and hopeful almost
as the entourage slips back indoors, where papers
will have been laid out on the mahogany table,
stacked on their own reflections. Politely
they sit down again to look at the terrible pictures.

Still life

Today there's a blind slop of oils
that stops before it's finished

where the ghost of a line trails
through an apple and an empty dish

to pull up exactly seven
inches from your eyes.

(Subversive, it says,
guerilla even.)

Where the woman sat
with streetlights to see by

once the sun sets,
you can open your eyes now:

a crumpled pink tissue, seven
shades of black and blue.

A prism

How long is it now since the two of us
stood watching the Irish Sea darken
with hardly a word between us?
I can barely recognise myself; your own
face is long gone,
leaving the sea unchanged behind it.

Things go on changing, all the same:
this morning, for instance,
the season loosens, and I walk away
from my seven colours, into
the forgetful light of spring,
as though, somehow, the new life

were really beginning here
and at last I had forgotten
the darkness waiting like a screen
behind and around me
where still, impossibly,
Richard of York gives battle in vain.

Tercets

Don't wake them; they have been asleep too long,
hooping each other with their open arms
and maybe dreaming. Anyway, leave them.

*

In the same room, saying next to nothing,
you start to hear every sound as it comes
back on itself, and imagine it changes.

*

If they dream of soldiers, are their dreams
cacophonous still with guns and shells, fire
ploughing up fields to sow them with the dead?

*

I can't see well in the dark, but it all
comes back in the end, and you whisper again
don't wake them now, they've been asleep too long.

The deaf wars

It's nearly over now.
I suppose you've broken cover,
though it makes no odds; the words
shrunk back, unspoken, long ago,
whatever you meant to say.
There's still maybe a year or two

to go before you tell
the whole truth, such as it is.
Tonight a soldier gets loaded
on a tranquilliser cocktail,
gaping at clouds of roses,
the silent blossoms of shells.

Charlie Chaplin went to France
To teach the cannibals how to dance
and here they come,
skipping over the trenches,
each one swinging a time-bomb.
And their theme today is silence.

So the mud has you washed up
on a final high place,
open-mouthed, amazed
in a stalled sign-language
for the last of the comic deaths.
Your smile trickles over the edge.

Totalled

The costumes are a kind of late-colonial,
all primary colours and designer labels;
the hair's worn long and blow-dried, accents
are half-way between here and America;
a badge on his lapel says the producer
won't take no for an answer, and maybe
it's true he has a way with the impossible:
resprayed old cars, given a last polish,
catapult into walls and shop-windows,
into each other, they're always totalled,
and right on cue the flames come bursting
just to make everything final;
the sound's dubbed later, of fists connecting,
gunshots, brakes, happy or sad music.

Two men are waiting in a skyline office,
each one silently adding up the other
and playing the razor-cool executive.
The first smoothes a map, points to one corner,
and thinks out all the disadvantages –
it's too late, and impossible anyway,
to make much of that sector. He's starting
to speak now, with a shrug in his voice
and his eyes fixed on the middle distance,
part of him slipping out to some margin
as a young achiever jokes in a monotone
of how already he's allowed for losses
and nowadays, in any case, that country
is washed-up, written-off, a place for dead people.

Count Dracula entertains (2)

A last dark rinse
and the dusk has gone, *the poetry*,
leaving me and the distance
alone here in our elements. Deny
me again, then again;
from you I'd expect no better, or worse.

In your lit town
the traffic goes all night, and keeps
you wide awake and sane
as, layer by layer, your head unwraps
itself like a present,
a book full of pictures both of us have seen.

(Rain at a slant
in the last of your dream-paintings
makes its oblique point
too late, now lies are waiting
under drab clouds
with stars and all the words for death coming out.)

Though dismal sods
like you, after a wife and a career,
who get ahead of the crowds
(of doubts? twinges that might be fear?)
still understand
enough of me to keep your Volvos on the roads,

you've never found
a way to what you really wanted,
the rights to your own ground
(your grandfathers were always dead
and the dead, like me,
are generous, carry nothing in their hands.)

And now the poetry,
my night collapsing round your ears
like a Gothic gallery
of stars and thunder, rain and bugbears.
You write a last
dark rinse for both of us: *the sky is a black sea.*

The third day
(for Michael Longley)

My head is melting;
smears of hair and flesh-tone
are slipping through the fingers
of hands that are no longer
just so much skin and bone,
and return to where they'd risen

on my grandfather's palette
in some makeshift studio,
a damp back-parlour
in Belfast or Glasgow.
Now, while the paint's wet,
he'll turn the street-corner

where my father might wait,
his hair shiny with Brylcreem,
to deliver another telegram
in forties London;
sucking on a boiled sweet,
there's nothing he foresees

that could bring him any closer
to his young son, the grandson,
whose unborn arms and legs
will have grown away from him
like the head that's melting now
with ice cream and Easter eggs.

The green, grassy slopes of the Boyne

Or, alternatively,
the Braniel Housing Estate.
The postman at the garden gate
hovers (except that, for me
there is no gate, and the garden
is grass rubbed dead, and dog turds)
hovers, and tells me he's no postman
(I never catch the exact words,
maybe it's a park-warden).
At any rate, he makes it known
that he has come today
no, to deliver nothing. To send away.

But nothing changes here, or never has:
a few times snow
has covered the whole garden. When I show
him the photographs of myself
standing up fat and smiling
against that year's white-out,
all he can do is look away again.
I pull him back, show him
the whole extent of change
in a garden that, in any case,
was never his to cultivate,
winter or summer, one step beyond the gate.

That Friday, looking down
at a city greyed out by smoke
rising with its own sound,
thud after thud, and all the time
a choir of sirens
swooping to work, I was standing
right at the very centre of the garden
while indoors the radio
announced, interpreted, till its voice broke.
The sun set as it always does, lighting
the hills and burning up clouds like rags.
They were gathering the dead in plastic bags.

This time, again, he's leading me
up that same garden path
to a familiar height, where I can see
down years, without any photograph,
to myself and others marching, beating
hard toy drums and dragging past
The green, grassy slopes of the Boyne.
When I come back
to the corner, I turn and start again.
The clouds are burning like photographs
all over again
and I turn around and go back, and around and back again.

Sunday in Great Tew
8th November 1987

1

It's time to get back to the car. Already, at half-past three,
the light's three-quarters gone, and back across the green
you can watch the shifting greys of a subtle fog by now
coming over to freeze the steps we leave, our ghosts' footprints,

to slight marks in November grass, and that's the last
of us this afternoon, this year, in this model village
a half-hour's drive from Oxford, where we come in summer
like the other tourists, to drink decent beer, sniff woodsmoke,

and admire thatched roofs on sturdy, stone-built houses,
as though the whole place were a replica of some England,
an idea on show, unchanging, glassy, not quite touchable.
But this is November, and Sunday. It is Sunday in Great Tew.

2

Every visit nowadays is an act of remembrance,
measuring changes in us against some other summer
when we sat here drinking, and swapped our random gossip
– friends, work and books, hard politics or love –

across a wooden table in an always busy pub
with proper beer on sale, not the watery Oxford slops,
and where, as their speciality, they sell hand-made pipes,
briars and clay-pipes, every one the genuine article,

(though these, admittedly, we never got around to buying);
one year we're talking about that headstrong, happy girl
you'd chased unluckily for months; another, and we're discussing
far-off acts of war, the real thing, here in the Falkland Arms.

3

The manor house, concealed behind thick trees and hedges,
might well be home now for some eccentric millionaire
who seldom shows his face; from the road going uphill
to the church, you can see through gaps down to the house itself,

heavy and strong, like the brash history it suggests,
having and holding so much; was it here since the Civil War,
when the bookish man who owned the place, Lord Falkland,
was a loyalist who found himself outmanoeuvred?

Once he played patron here to the poet Abraham Cowley
– outmanoeuvred himself, in his way, by Parliament's
staunch worker Milton, true to different lights, but blind,
po-faced, pig-headed and holy, almost an Ulsterman.

4

Names of the wars change, and of course the protagonists change:
the church contains its various slabs of memorial stone
with names of the dead men, where today a single wreath
of poppies does its duty, pays them its stiff homage

of glaring red flowers for death, rootless and papery,
bunched together in grief or pride, or with indifference,
on a Sunday like any other Sunday in November;
there's a smell of damp mixed with the smell of genteel ladies

and the cold slips forward from the walls and the dark floor
so that here, too, we must become aliens, shut out
from whatever we might be tempted to call our own, reminded
that the dead are close, that here the poppy is an English flower.

5

There are no words to find for the dead, and no gestures,
no sermons to be turned, no curses to lay now and for ever
on one house, or the other, or on both; there is no need
to rerun the scalding images they have left in our keeping,

or pitch hot misery into this cold comfort, as though
one ill-bred outburst here might make sense of it;
there is no need to watch television in the afternoon
to understand that nobody has ever died with a good reason,

and see the Irish slaughter one another like wogs;
there is no need, only now a blinding appetite,
this afternoon, tomorrow, the day after; so tonight in the Killyhevlin
Hotel the team from ITN will be ordering champagne.

6

One drink today, one pint of beer, and one short walk
in the sober afternoon around an English village,
a conversation jumping from one silence to another
in ripe Oxonian vowels, two figures on their own

in some pretend backwater with picture-postcard views,
slipping discreetly into a proper country churchyard
and quoting poetry, and laughing now that everything's
too late, imagining the right history for the place,

inglorious, largely mute: two generals discussing terms,
their fists set hard on the oak table that's between them,
where neither will say the word 'defeat', though both return
with different names for victory to their beaten people.

7

Even in the middle of winter, the sky is everywhere,
folded above us as we walk with hands sunk in our pockets,
our fingers worrying over cold coins and key-rings;
it covers us completely as a numbing anaesthetic

so that every time we might look up, the two of us,
the trees we can see with fog trailing in their branches,
the scarecrow standing up in its one blank field
(or what looks from here like a scarecrow), the row of old houses

snug and expensive and empty, even the pub behind us,
all become incidental, oblique marks set in the margin,
swept out to the edges of a single, clear perspective,
the one that matters most, or least, and never changes.

8

A flower of crumpled paper with its button of black plastic
has fallen from somebody's coat, and is lying here beside
a vacant phone-box opposite the village school
along with an empty packet of twenty Benson and Hedges

and what looks like a bus-ticket; such modest litter
might be the last thing you notice, and for all the cars parked
there's nobody here but us walking out in the open,
and even we are making our way back to a car,

opening, closing doors, clicking in seat-belts, switching on
dipped headlights and starting the engine; turning around
and taking a right at the deserted school,
on our way home, leaving absolutely nothing behind us.

Peter McDonald was born in 1962 in Belfast, and was educated at Methodist College, Belfast and University College, Oxford. He has been a Junior Research Fellow of Christ Church, Oxford, and is now Fellow and Lecturer in English at Pembroke College, Cambridge.

Selections of his poetry were published in Blackstaff's *Trio Poetry 3* anthology in 1982 and in *New Chatto Poets* in 1986. He won the Newdigate Prize in 1983, and an Eric Gregory Award in 1987.

His critical book, *Louis MacNeice: the poet in his contexts*, is published by Oxford University Press. He is married and lives in Cambridge.